12 THINGS TO KNOW ABOUT
FRACKING

by Rebecca Felix

12 STORY LIBRARY

www.12StoryLibrary.com

12-Story Library is an imprint of Peterson Publishing Company and Press Room Editions.

Produced for 12-Story Library by Red Line Editorial

Photographs ©: Ralph Wilson/AP Images, cover, 1, 20; Brennan Linsley/AP Images, 4, 12; Mark Steil/AP Images, 5; Thinkstock, 6, 18, 24, 28; Library of Congress, 7; Shutterstock Images, 8, 11, 26, 29; Dale G. Young/AP Images, 9; Sheri Armstrong/Shutterstock Images, 10; Pat Sullivan/AP Images, 13; Keith Srakocic/AP Images, 15; Lauren Donovan/AP Images, 16; Steve Oehlenschlager/Shutterstock Images, 17; Design Pics/Thinkstock, 19; Steven Frame/Shutterstock Images, 21; Philip Lange/Shutterstock Images, 22; Fedor Selivanov/Shutterstock Images, 23; Les Stone/Corbis, 25; Brian Brown Images/Thinkstock, 27

ISBN
978-1-63235-029-9 (hardcover)
978-1-63235-089-3 (paperback)
978-1-62143-070-4 (hosted ebook)

Library of Congress Control Number: 2014946817

Printed in the United States of America
Mankato, MN
October, 2014

12
STORY
LIBRARY

Go beyond the book. Get free, up-to-date content on this topic at 12StoryLibrary.com.

TABLE OF CONTENTS

FRACKING IS SHORT FOR "HYDRAULIC FRACTURING"

Fracking is a process used in oil drilling. It breaks up underground rock to free the oil and natural gas inside. Oil and natural gas are fossil fuels. They provide energy when burned. Fossil fuels are used to power vehicles, heat buildings and homes, and provide electricity.

The fracking process begins with drilling vertical wells. These wells are drilled until a deep rock layer called shale is reached. Then the

Drilling for natural gas in Colorado

well is drilled horizontally into the shale. Many shale wells are between 6,000 and 10,000 feet (1,800 and 3,100 m) deep.

39

Percentage of US natural gas extracted from shale in 2012.

- Fracking is blasting water, chemicals, and sand into drilled wells to break shale.
- Fracking frees oil and natural gas from underground rock. People collect it and use it for energy.
- Today's fracking process includes horizontal drilling and wells.

Once drilling is complete, the fracking process begins. Millions of gallons of high-pressure water are blasted down the well into the rock. The blast makes fractures in the shale. This frees the oil or gas trapped inside. Chemicals are mixed with the water used to create the fracture. These chemicals get rid of bacteria and minerals in the rock. These small things might keep the oil or gas from flowing. Fracking water is also mixed with sand. The sand keeps the fractures open so gas or oil will keep flowing out. The oil or gas rises up the well. It is collected and sold to companies for energy use.

A FRACKING BOOM BEGAN IN THE 2000s

Oil and gas companies began fracking in the 1940s. These technologies were not common, however, until the 1980s. In the 1990s, advanced technology allowed companies to drill deeper wells. They could also be more precise. This allowed horizontal drilling of shale. The shale held great amounts of oil and natural gas.

Technology and techniques continued to improve. Oil and natural gas companies discovered large US shale formations. A large one is under Pennsylvania, New York, West Virginia, Maryland, and Ohio. Another is under Montana and North Dakota. In the 2000s, a

A fracking well in North Dakota

US oil and natural gas boom began. One energy expert called 2003 the "the key year" in fracking. The first horizontal drill was used that year. It proved fracking was possible. By the end of 2003, 1,900 horizontal US fracking wells were in operation. Ten years later, the US Department of Energy said "at least 2 million" oil and gas wells had been fracked.

THE FIRST US OIL WELL AND DRILLING BOOM

Edwin Drake drilled the first US oil well in Pennsylvania in 1859. Drake drilled into a natural oil seep. This is a spot where oil already rises up out of the ground naturally. The drilled well was lined with pipe. The well was a success. It produced 20 to 40 barrels per day. People began to drill wells around the country. A US oil boom period began.

8 million

Gallons of water, on average, used by each horizontal fracture in a fracking well.

- Earlier drilling and fracking accessed shallow rock.
- Shale is very hard and deep rock.
- Horizontally fracking shale freed great amounts of natural gas and oil.
- A US oil and gas boom began in the 2000s.

Edwin Drake's first oil well in Pennsylvania

FOSSIL FUELS SPEED UP CLIMATE CHANGE

The fracking boom has freed new and great amounts of fossil fuels. People use fossil fuels for energy for many reasons. Natural gas is plentiful. It powers many things and is easy to store. Oil shares these qualities. Gasoline is made from oil. Most vehicles run on gasoline.

But burning fossil fuels is not good for the environment. Doing so gives off greenhouse gases. These are gases that collect in the atmosphere. Earth gets energy from the sun. Some is absorbed. The rest is meant to bounce back into space, outside Earth's atmosphere. But greenhouse gases trap this energy. This speeds up climate change. Environmental changes are set in motion. These changes can negatively affect Earth's weather and environments.

Carbon dioxide is a greenhouse gas. It is released when humans

Fossil fuels release pollution into the atmosphere.

Natural gas burns off a fracking well.

burn natural gas and oil. Burning natural gas gives off less carbon dioxide than burning oil. But natural gas is mostly made up of methane. It is a greenhouse gas 34 times stronger than carbon dioxide. If natural gas leaks before it is burned, it releases methane. Using fossil fuels releases a lot of greenhouse gases. This has a negative effect on the environment.

7,193
Million short tons (6,526 metric tons) of greenhouse gases released in the United States in 2012.

- Natural gas and oil release greenhouse gases when burned.
- Natural gas is made of mostly methane.
- Methane is a very strong greenhouse gas.
- Greenhouse gases speed up climate change. This leads to negative effects around the world.

WAYS CLIMATE CHANGE AFFECTS EARTH

Climate change can affect Earth's weather, animals, plants, people, and oceans. Greenhouse gases trap heat and energy in the atmosphere. This causes temperatures to rise. Sea levels rise as glaciers melt. It can lead to extreme weather such as wildfires and floods. These events can cause plant life and ecosystems to change. The amount of food and water available for animals and humans can also change.

FRACKING CONTRIBUTES TO CLIMATE CHANGE, TOO

The fuels produced by fracking can be harmful to the environment. But the process of fracking also can be damaging. Fracking and drilling involve many machines and vehicles. They dig up the earth at drilling sites, provide power to wells, and haul oil and gas. Many run on fuel made from oil. This adds carbon to the air, speeding up climate change.

Some companies have found ways to avoid this. Machines can run on fuel such as natural gas

Fracking uses a lot of heavy equipment, including tanker trucks.

that releases less carbon. But buying new machinery can be expensive. Using natural gas can still contribute to climate change. Natural gas releases carbon when it is burned. Methane is released if natural gas leaks during transport or refueling. Fracked wells can also have methane leaks. This is a major environmental concern. Fracked gas wells leak 40 to 60 percent more methane than non-fracked wells. Drilling companies are working to stop these leaks. Many can be fixed just by making sure a well's bolts are tight and seals are not worn out. Special cameras have also been invented. They can spot methane leaks. But they are an expensive solution. One camera can cost up to $100,000.

450,000

Approximate short tons (408,200 metric tons) of air pollution released annually in the United States from fracking.

- Trucks and machines used in fracking release carbon dioxide.
- Methane can leak during natural gas collection.
- Many drilling companies are powering machines and trucks with natural gas.
- Companies are finding ways to prevent methane leaks.

Older oil wells do not leak methane as often as fracking wells do.

FRACKING USES—AND WASTES—A LOT OF WATER

One fracking well can require 7 million gallons (27 million L) of water. Many other industries use a lot of water, too. But most can return the used water to the environment again. Fracking water is called wastewater. It is contaminated by fracking chemicals. It cannot be returned to nature. In 2012 fracking in the United States created approximately 280 billion gallons (787 billion L) of wastewater. That is enough to fill more than 424,200 Olympic-sized swimming pools!

About 30 percent of wastewater stays underground. The rest rises or gets pumped to the surface. Usually it then gets shipped to other sites. There it

Oil rig workers on a fracking well's water tanks

600

Average number of chemicals found in fracking wastewater.

- US oil and natural gas companies created 280 billions of gallons of fracking wastewater in 2012.
- Some companies are developing gels to replace the water used in fracking.
- 55 percent of US fracking wells are found in areas suffering from drought.

An organization that studies climate change published a fracking report in 2014. It said 55 percent of US fracking wells are in areas suffering from drought. It is already hard to find enough water to drink or for farming in these areas. Many people are upset that water they could use for these things is used for fracking instead.

is injected deep underground for permanent storage. Companies are looking for ways to reduce their water use. Some are using a gel instead of water. Others are finding ways to recycle wastewater. They use the water to frack again. But some experts believe the water saved by recycling will not be enough to make up for the great amount needed for future fracking.

Jars containing fracking wastewater (right) and recycled water

SOME FRACKING CHEMICALS REMAIN SECRET

The chemicals used in fracking vary by company and region. Companies use chemicals to help break up minerals in the rock. They also use chemicals to keep fracking water flowing. The US government is not responsible for regulating fracking companies. Each state handles regulation separately. Many companies list the chemicals they use on FracFocus.org. But they are not required by law to list all the chemicals. They can keep some secret so other companies cannot copy their chemical combinations.

750
Number of chemicals used in fracking according to a 2013 survey.

- Fracking companies use chemicals in their water solutions.
- Companies do not have to tell the public about all the chemicals they use.
- Many people are concerned that chemicals used in fracking can make them sick.
- There have been proven cases of fracking chemicals causing illness in people who live near wells.

THINK ABOUT IT

Do you think fracking companies should be allowed to keep some chemicals secret? Would your answer change if a fracking well was near your home? Or if you owned a fracking company?

A worker tests wastewater in Beaver Falls, Pennsylvania, for fracking chemicals.

DOES FRACKING MAKE PEOPLE SICK?

Some fracking companies use chemicals known to cause cancer. Research showed some water sources near fracked wells contained chemicals that could cause birth defects. Air pollution from fracking can also make people sick. It can cause asthma, eye irritation, and other health problems.

But keeping secrets makes the public distrust companies. Many people think companies keep some chemicals secret because they are dangerous or make people sick. People living near wells fear chemicals will leak into groundwater. Cases of wastewater chemicals in drinking water sources have been reported from Pennsylvania to New Mexico.

Baker Hughes is a US fracking company. In April 2014, it said it would share the names of all chemicals it uses. This was to build trust with the public. But there was a catch. The company would share only in areas where oil and gas customers supported its doing so. But many still felt the decision to share was a positive step. In 2014 the Environmental Protection Agency considered making national rules about sharing chemicals.

FRACKING HAS TRANSFORMED TOWNS AND STATES

The United States has several large shale formations. The Bakken is one of the largest. It is in Montana and North Dakota. It may hold up to 4.3 billion barrels of oil. The Bakken was discovered in 1951. But people could not get to its oil until horizontal fracking was invented.

Fracking the Bakken has changed North Dakota. Many towns there used to be small, with few people.

LIVING IN A NORTH DAKOTA BOOM TOWN

Some boom towns end up with a lot of men living there. Male workers move to work oil or gas wells. Many do not move with their families. They live in camps with other working men. Families that do move to boom towns find schools are overcrowded. Some live in campers with other families because there is no housing.

RVs parked in the Williston, North Dakota, Wal-Mart parking lot.

Some have become big cities since the oil boom. Fracking has also brought a lot of money to North Dakota towns. Businesses stay busy. Almost everyone has a job. Roads are being fixed. People have built new businesses and homes in these places.

But there has not been enough housing for everyone who has moved there. Camps have been set up for oil field workers. Other workers become homeless. They live in their cars. In 2012 many were even living in a Wal-Mart parking lot.

The Marcellus is another huge US natural gas shale formation. Pennsylvania has been the center of the Marcellus fracking boom.

9.3
Percentage increase in the population of Williston, North Dakota, from 2011 to 2012.

- Fracking wells have created boom towns in some states.
- Not all boom towns have enough housing.
- Fracking wells can bring in lots of money to towns.

Towns there have changed in ways similar to those in North Dakota. There is more traffic and noise. More people have moved in. Some people have wells or huge fracking sites in their backyards. The landscape has been scarred and dug up. However, there have also been boosts to local businesses and the economy.

Fracking wells can make a big impact on the landscape around them.

MANY FRACKING WELLS ARE ON PRIVATE PROPERTY

In March 2014, 15 million Americans lived within 1 mile (1.6 km) of a fracking well drilled since the year 2000. Many wells are on property owned by private citizens, not oil companies. In North Dakota, 90 percent of wells are on private property. Landowners can make a lot of money if they own the rights to the minerals on their properties. They receive money from the company that builds a well there as long as the well keeps giving out gas or oil.

But not all people own the rights to their underground land. Sometimes one person or group owns the rights to land above ground. Another owns rights to the minerals and resources

This fracking well is on a Colorado farm.

under that land. Sometimes companies can even drill without permission. Laws allow this in 39 states. These laws allow companies to drill underground from one property into another piece of land. They can do this even if landowners do not want them to.

Some who agree to have their land fracked end up wishing they had not. Fracking creates a lot of noise. There are almost always pumps working. Trucks haul oil and gas, lights are on all the time, and traffic increases. The risk of exposure to chemicals and air pollution is high as well.

1/3

Estimated fraction of all mineral rights in the United States owned by local, state, and federal governments.

- Many wells are on private property.
- If people own mineral rights to their land, they can make a lot of money from wells built there.
- Some people do not own the rights to the minerals under their land.

Trucks haul oil and gas from fracking wells through the night.

OIL AND GAS PRODUCTION BOOSTS THE ECONOMY

Williston, North Dakota, is the center of the Bakken oil boom. In 2013 its population was 16,000 people. At the same time, there were more than 40,000 oil jobs available there. The oil and gas boom created 1.7 million US jobs between 2008 and 2012. Experts predict 3 million more jobs will be created by 2020.

US oil and gas production also boosts the US economy. In 2013 the country spent about $300 billion on foreign oil. If it could produce enough of its own oil, that money could stay

Fracking companies provide many jobs.

79.25

Percentage growth in wages in Pennsylvania's oil and gas industry between 2002 and 2012.

- Producing oil and gas in the United States boosts the country's economy.
- It also keeps United States gas prices low.
- US oil and natural gas production keeps oil prices stable.

in the US economy. Fracking natural gas helps the US economy, too. Having so much of this resource can reduce its price. This allows more people to buy and use it. The money stays in the United States. While US oil production helps the economy, it does not make oil cheaper. But it does keep prices from changing too much. Oil prices are set worldwide. More oil being produced in the United States means more oil for all countries. This keeps the price from going up or down too much.

Oil tanker cars transport oil and natural gas from the United States.

FRACKING INCREASES ENERGY INDEPENDENCE

The United States gets a lot of its oil from other countries. It has done so for a long time. Several of these countries are in the Middle East. Many people in the United States feel the country should try to become energy independent. They want the United States to produce all of the energy it uses. This would keep the United States from being involved in conflicts over foreign oil.

The United States has become less dependent on foreign oil. This is due in part to the fracking boom. The country can get more of its oil at home. But it still has to import oil from other countries. The International Energy Agency believes this could change in the future, though. It said the United

The Middle Eastern country of Bahrain produces oil.

84

Percentage of energy use in the United States fulfilled by domestic energy sources in 2012.

- The United States uses energy resources from other countries.
- The United States may be the leading oil and gas producer by 2016.
- Extracting its own oil helps keep the United States out of some conflicts.

States could meet all its own energy needs by 2035.

The large amount of natural gas now available through fracking

WORLD'S TOP OIL AND GAS PRODUCER?

Saudi Arabia has produced the most oil in the world for many years. But some energy experts say the United States will produce more by 2016. The boom has made the country close to top in oil and gas for the first time in a long time.

will also play a role in US energy independence. In 2014 President Barack Obama said it brought the country "closer to energy independence than we've been in decades."

Saudi Arabia is one of the world's top oil producers.

FRACKING IS BANNED IN SOME PLACES

Pittsburgh, Pennsylvania, was the first city to ban fracking in 2010. Cities in Colorado, Texas, and Ohio have done the same since. Mora County in New Mexico was the first county to ban fracking in 2013. In 2014 a county council on Hawaii's main island voted on whether to allow fracking there. It took them less than three minutes to decide to ban it.

The entire state of New York has had a moratorium on fracking since 2008. New Yorkers elected a new governor in 2011. He said the ban will last at least until 2015. This has created much debate. New York lies within the Marcellus formation. It may hold enough gas to power all US homes for 50 years. Some believe the country's future energy plans

Pittsburgh, Pennsylvania, banned fracking in 2010.

depend on the whole Marcellus being fracked.

California may be the next state to ban fracking. In May 2014, a bill was gaining support to place a moratorium on fracking. Kathryn Phillips, director of the environmental organization Sierra Club California, hoped just considering it would be enough to stop fracking. She said, "Just the threat of a moratorium discourages investment."

People protest fracking in New York.

THINK ABOUT IT

Are there fracking wells in your town? How do you feel about them? If there are none, how would you feel if some were built? List a few ways fracking has changed or could change your town.

423
Number of state and local measures taken against fracking.

- Cities and counties have passed laws banning fracking.
- New York State has a moratorium on fracking until at least 2015.
- Some believe fracking bans will hurt future US energy plans.

FRACKING MAY BECOME CLEANER AND SAFER

Many people agree fracking is not going to stop or slow down any time soon. Because of this, some want to make fracking safer and cleaner. Many drilling companies are working toward this goal. They are recycling fracking water. Some are replacing dangerous chemicals with less harsh alternatives. They are

CLEAN AND RENEWABLE ENERGIES

Renewable means to be restored naturally. Solar energy is energy from sunlight. It is a renewable energy. There is always more sunlight. It cannot be used up. Wind energy is also renewable. Wind cannot be used up. These energies are also clean energies. They do not give off greenhouse gases or pollution.

Solar panels collect energy from the sun's rays.

using machines and vehicles that run on renewable energy, such as solar power.

Many people want renewable energies to become the country's top energy sources. Great amounts of oil and natural gas are now available through fracking. But using them will continue to speed up climate change. Fossil fuels are a finite resource. One day they will run out.

It may be a long time before renewable energies are widely used. Until then natural gas may be used as an energy bridge. Experts and others in the energy industry have said it could be used to get the country on its way to using renewable energies. The future of

27
Percentage of electricity generated from natural gas in the United States in 2013.

- Some people would like the United States to rely more on renewable energy sources.
- Natural gas could be the bridge between fossil fuel use and renewable energy use.
- Fracking has changed the history of energy in the United States.

fracking will depend on people. Fracking may become widely banned. Or the boom may continue. Either way, it has already changed US energy history.

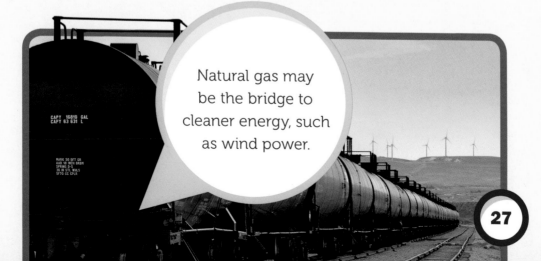

Natural gas may be the bridge to cleaner energy, such as wind power.

CAPY 16810 GAL
CAPY 63 631 L

MARK 50 9FT GR
AAR 10 INCH BRGN
SPRING D-5
36 IN STL WULS
5F70 CC CPLR

FACT SHEET

- Shale is a hard rock layer located deep in the earth. It is below other rock layers that are softer or have more holes. Several of the large or major shale deposits being fracked today were discovered long ago. But people were not able to drill and frack them effectively. Today an oil and natural gas boom is occurring because of advances in technology that allowed shale horizontal fracking to succeed.

- Fracking is the main process used to access shale gas and oil. It has become controversial for those opposed to gathering and using these fuels. But fracking is not the only technology that has unearthed new sources of oil and gas. Fracking and horizontal drilling *together* are the key to new deposits being available. These technologies have existed together for many decades. But they have recently been perfected and advanced.

- People oppose fracking for several reasons. Fracking and drilling processes add to climate change. They emit greenhouse gases that trap energy in Earth's atmosphere. Burning natural gas and oil for energy also adds to climate change. The advances in horizontal fracking have allowed a lot more of these fossil fuels to be accessed. This equals a lot more greenhouse gases that will be released in the environment as they are used.

- Fracking helps the United States become more energy independent. The United States has relied on foreign oil sources for a long time. Many of these sources are in the Middle East. Being dependent on foreign oil can create problems. In 1973, several Middle Eastern countries used their oil to show power. They limited the amount of gas they sold to the United States. There was not enough gas for people to fill their cars. Becoming more energy independent would help the United States avoid these types of situations. Oil production from fracking increases US energy independence.

GLOSSARY

absorbed
Soaked up.

atmosphere
The mass of air that surrounds Earth.

drought
A long dry spell.

economy
The system of making, selling, and buying things.

ecosystems
All living things in an environment.

finite resource
Energy sources that cannot be restored naturally.

fossil fuels
Fuels created over millions of years from remains of dead plants and animals.

fractures
Makes cracks or breaks in something.

import
To bring a product in from another country.

moratorium
A set time when something is banned.

precise
Accurate, very neat, and exact.

regulating
Controlling, managing, or making laws for something.

renewable energies
Energy sources that can be restored naturally.

rights
Things a person is legally allowed or deserves.

FOR MORE INFORMATION

Books

Bailey, Diane. *Natural Gas Power*. Mankato, MN: Creative Education, 2014. Print.

Caduto, Michael J. *Catch the Wind, Harness the Sun*. North Adams, MA: Storey Publishing, 2011. Print.

Nagelhout, Ryan. *Fracking*. New York: Gareth Stevens, 2014. Print.

Websites

Energy Kids: Natural Gas Basics
www.eia.gov/kids/energy.cfm?page=natural_gas_home-basics

Energy Kids: Oil (Petroleum) Basics
www.eia.gov/KIDS/energy.cfm?page=oil_home-basics-k.cfm

Nick News: "What's the Deal With Fracking?"
www.nick.com/videos/clip/nick-news-136-full-episode.html

Tiki the Penguin: Tiki's Quick Guide to Fracking
www.tiki.oneworld.net/fracking/fracking.html

INDEX

About the Author

Rebecca Felix is a writer and editor from Minnesota. She has written and edited books for kids on all kinds of topics. These include fairy tales, manners, states, animals, weather, and space.

READ MORE FROM 12-STORY LIBRARY

Every 12-Story Library book is available in many formats, including Amazon Kindle and Apple iBooks. For more information, visit your device's store or 12StoryLibrary.com.